P9-CFR-284

THOMAS JEFFERSON

CHARLES PATTERSON

THOMAS JEFFERSON

FRANKLIN WATTS
NEW YORK / LONDON / TORONTO / SYDNEY
A FIRST BOOK / 1987

Cover photograph courtesy of
The Granger Collection, New York.

All other photographs courtesy of
The Collections of the Library of Congress.

Library of Congress Cataloging-in-Publication Data

Patterson, Charles.
Thomas Jefferson.

(A First book)
Bibliography: p.
Includes index.
Summary: Examines the life, political career, and
achievements of the third president of the United States,
including a discussion of his beliefs and their influence
on the Declaration of Independence.
1. Jefferson, Thomas, 1743-1826—Juvenile literature.
2. Presidents—United States—Biography—Juvenile
literature. [1. Jefferson, Thomas, 1743-1826.
2. Presidents] I. Title.
E332.79.P323 1987   973.4′6′0924 [B]   [92] 86-23361
ISBN 0-531-10306-4

For Dave, Bob and Alice
and their families

CONTENTS

THOMAS JEFFERSON

PREFACE

For more than half a century, Thomas Jefferson was at the center of American history. He entered politics as a champion of the revolutionary cause in Virginia. Then, in the Continental Congress, he wrote the Declaration of Independence when he was thirty-three. After serving as the American ambassador in France, he returned to the United States to play an important part in the first decades of the new country.

Under George Washington, he was America's first Secretary of State. During the presidency of John Adams, he was vice president. During his own years as president from 1801 to 1809, he healed the wounds of a divided nation, kept the peace, and doubled the size of the United States. Even after his retirement, the influence of his ideas and example continued during the administrations of the next two presidents, his longtime friends from Virginia, James Madison and James Monroe.

Thomas Jefferson was also a man of immense talent and learning. His brilliant mind was respected in Europe as well as America. He was interested in just about everything —philosophy, architecture, science—and his personal library was probably the best in America. He was an intellectual giant—a champion of ideas and a passionate defender of freedom of thought and belief. All his life he fought for the right of a person to learn, think, worship freely, and seek the truth. He also opposed the forces of oppression, ignorance, dogmatism, fear, and superstition. Jefferson's dream of creating a great university that embodied these principles came true toward the end of his life, when he founded the University of Virginia in Charlottesville.

The many intellectual and political contributions that Thomas Jefferson made to the life and history of the United States remain an impressive part of the fabric of our national life to this day.

BOYHOOD

—1—

Thomas Jefferson was born on April 13, 1743, in what was then the British colony of Virginia. His father was Peter Jefferson, whose ancestors had come across the Atlantic Ocean from Wales in Britain three generations earlier. Peter married Jane Randolph, who had been born in England. They moved into the wilderness of western Virginia and bought choice land on the Rivanna River. There Peter Jefferson cleared and farmed the land, and he built a simple wooden house, which he named Shadwell.

Peter and Jane Jefferson had two daughters before their first son, Thomas, was born. Shadwell was surrounded by steep wooded hillsides and thick forests where the wolves howled at night. All his life Thomas Jefferson loved the woods, rivers, hills, and mountains of this part of Virginia—what later became Albemarle County. After he grew up, he settled down in this same area and called it home for the rest of his life.

When Thomas was two years old, his father moved the family fifty miles away to an older and better house called Tuckahoe. Peter Jefferson and his best friend, William Randolph, had agreed that if anything happened to one of them, the other one would look after the other's family and property. So when Randolph died at the age of thirty-three and left behind three children—two daughters and a boy, also named Thomas—Peter Jefferson put someone in charge of Shadwell and moved his family to Tuckahoe. There Thomas Jefferson was part of the combined family of six children.

Although Tuckahoe was in a more thickly settled area on the James River, it was still surrounded by the exciting world of the wilderness. William Randolph had more than a hundred slaves, so Thomas got used to playing and growing up with black children. His father had had some slaves at Shadwell, but not as many. At Tuckahoe, for every white person there were nine blacks. Jefferson enjoyed the company of his black friends, but he got his first lesson in the ways of slavery when he discovered that only the white children could go to school.

Thomas began to read and write at the age of five, when his father turned him over to the family's hired tutor. His father taught him how to ride a horse and use a gun. Once Thomas's father sent him into the woods alone with a rifle to make him learn how to survive on his own in the wilderness.

When Thomas was nine, his father took the family back to Shadwell. But Thomas didn't go with them. Instead, he went off to school five miles from Tuckahoe, where, along with a few other students, he boarded with his teacher's family. Although Thomas didn't like his teacher very much, he spent five years with him learning Latin, Greek, and French. He was able to go home and live with the rest of his family at Shadwell only during the summer.

Thomas admired his father, and, while Mr. Jefferson was alive, Thomas learned many things from him. Peter Jefferson was big and very strong. He once pulled down a shed with a rope that three other men had failed to bring down. He could upend huge, heavy barrels all by himself.

Peter Jefferson was also a leader and a respected member of his community. At different times, he served as sheriff, judge, justice of the peace, member of the Virginia House of Burgesses, and lieutenant colonel in the militia. He was also a good friend of the Indians as well as a skilled surveyor and mapmaker who made long trips over the mountains into the wilderness. Thomas loved to hear the stories his father brought back about coming close to starvation and meeting wild bears. The map of western Virginia that Peter Jefferson and another man made was used for many years afterward. And he worked hard to raise a family of eleven children—the three Randolph children as well as his own family of six girls and two boys.

Thomas was fourteen when his father died. Knowing his son's curiosity and love of learning, Peter Jefferson left him his personal library of forty-two books, his bookcase, his desk, and his mathematical instruments. In his will he left Shadwell to his wife, Jane, and divided up the rest of his slaves and money among his eight children, to be theirs when they came of age. He divided the rest of his land between his two sons. When Thomas reached twenty-one, he was to inherit thirty slaves and more than 2,500 acres.

Later Jefferson wrote that his father's education had been "quite neglected, but being of a strong mind, sound judgment, and eager after information, he read much and improved himself." Although Peter Jefferson didn't have as much time for his own education as he would have liked, his respect for books and education got his son off to a good start.

YOUNG MAN

—2—

After his father's death, Jefferson attended the little school of the Reverend James Maury, closer to home. During the week he and the four other students boarded with the clergyman's family, but Saturdays he spent home at Shadwell. Maury was severe but learned. With his help Jefferson learned to read the ancient classics in their original Greek and Latin. Thomas and the other students became such good friends that they remained friends for the rest of their lives. Thomas's best friend, Dabney Carr, later married his younger sister, Martha. During these two years at Reverend Maury's, Jefferson also improved his riding and learned to dance and play the violin.

In 1760, at the age of seventeen, Thomas Jefferson came down out of the hills of western Virginia to attend the College of William and Mary in the capital of Williamsburg. Williamsburg was the political center of the Virginia colony and a bustling city when compared to Shadwell. The British royal governor lived there and the House of Burgesses met there as well. But Jefferson was more interested in his studies than he was in politics. He spent most of the day and much of the night reading.

He lived, ate, and studied at the college, but he wasn't just a bookworm. Soon he made friends with three older men. The first was William Small, the professor of mathematics and natural history at the college, who became his primary teacher. Until his return to England, Small was like a father to Jefferson. He introduced Thomas to George Wythe, who later became Jefferson's law teacher and life-long friend. Wythe, in turn, introduced Jefferson into the company of the popular royal governor, Francis Fauquier. All three men liked the serious young student, and they often invited him to join them for dinner.

At nineteen Jefferson began his study of law under Wythe and lived in town rather than at the college. He also began spending longer stretches of time at Shadwell, where he could do his reading while he managed the family farms. He read widely in several areas, not just law, and kept ordering books for his expanding library. Later, Wythe would leave Jefferson all his books in his will because he knew how much Jefferson loved reading. When Jefferson came across something important in his reading, he copied it into his notebooks.

When he was in Williamsburg, Jefferson went to parties and spent time with his friends. He was tall and lean, but a bit shy and awkward, and not especially handsome. He had reddish hair, hazel eyes, and skin that freckled and burned easily in the sun. He did have good manners and a gift for intelligent conversation. After he began getting invited to the palace for dinner with his three older friends, he dressed less like a student and more like a young gentleman. By this time he was already a skilled horseman and a fine musician. He practiced on his violin a couple of hours every day, and every week he joined other amateur musicians at the palace for a concert.

Jefferson was nineteen when he fell in love with a charming, pretty sixteen-year-old by the name of Rebecca Burwell. When she gave him her profile cut out of black paper, he carried it around in his watchcase. However, he seems to have spent more time and energy writing about her to a friend than he did in talking to her directly. His letters show that he was unhappy, confused, and certain that she didn't like him as much as he liked her. Whenever he did get the chance to visit or talk with her, he was tongue-tied and unsure of himself. He was obviously not ready to get married. Before long she did what he was sure she would do all along—she married someone else.

Jefferson got his first taste of colonial politics by seeing his friend and teacher George Wythe in action. At the opposite end of town from the college, the capitol building housed the General Court, where Wythe practiced law, and the House of Burgesses, where Wythe was also a respected member. There Jefferson also got to see the other colonial leaders.

One of them, a young, self-taught lawyer by the name of Patrick Henry, impressed Jefferson very much. In 1765, after Britain passed the Stamp Act, which imposed new taxes on the American colonies, Jefferson went to the capitol to hear the debate. Standing at the door of the chamber, Jefferson heard Henry's fiery speech against the

Stamp Act. Many of the older delegates felt that Henry went too far, but Jefferson, then twenty-two, was impressed and moved by Henry's blistering attack on the king and British policy.

The next year Jefferson got his first chance to travel outside the colony of Virginia. Besides travel, one of the reasons for his trip was to have himself inoculated against smallpox, a procedure then illegal in Virginia. Jefferson remained a lifelong champion of this enlightened practice. His three-month journey to the north took him to Annapolis, Maryland, where he visited the lower house of that colony's Assembly while it was in session. He also traveled to the busy port cities of Philadelphia and New York. Then he returned by sea to Virginia. After finally completing his long course of legal studies with Wythe, Jefferson was admitted to the state bar, which licensed him to practice law.

LAW AND
MARRIAGE

—3—

Although Jefferson was always more interested in studying law than in practicing it, he did build up a good practice over the next seven years. Even though the uncertainty of getting paid on time—or at all—was a constant problem, Jefferson took nearly a thousand cases. He had to travel by horse over the back roads and trails to the General Court at Williamsburg and to county courts closer to home to maintain contacts with clients.

At Shadwell, he was head of the family. As the oldest son, his job was to manage the family farms and keep the account books. He also had to take care of his mother and the four children who were still at home—a younger, unmarried sister, who was retarded; another sister, who would soon leave to get married; and the twins, who were only twelve.

Jefferson's oldest sister, Jane, had always been his favorite. His two other sisters, Mary and Martha, had both gotten married and left Shadwell, but Jane did not marry. She loved music and had a wonderful voice. In the evening she and Thomas used to go down to the river and sing, while he played his violin. She was his most cherished companion at Shadwell, but this closeness ended in 1765 when Jane died. She was twenty-five.

Two years after he started his law practice, Jefferson followed in his father's footsteps by getting elected to the House of Burgesses. When the new British governor dismissed the old Assembly and called for new elections, the voters of Albemarle County (only white males who owned land could vote) elected Jefferson one of their two burgesses. In May, 1769, he went to Williamsburg to take up his duties as a legislator and begin what proved to be a long and eventful career in politics.

Jefferson's elders recognized his talent early, so they gave him many assignments. At the larger meetings he hardly ever spoke up, but he was industrious and productive on committees. Because of his skill in writing laws and drafting resolutions, he was given much paperwork to do. Fortunately, this was the kind of work he liked best.

His first act as a legislator was to introduce a bill that would make it easier to free slaves. Like many Virginia families, his owned slaves. He had grown up with them, and his father left his to him and to his other children in his will. However, Jefferson had always disliked slavery and wanted to improve the condition of his own slaves. He thought the law that made it illegal to set slaves free should be changed, but his bill got nowhere because Jefferson's ideas about slavery were much too far ahead of his time. In his law practice, he once took the case of a slave of mixed race who thought he should be free because he had a white grandmother. Jefferson agreed with him, and in his brief he included the words: "Under the law of nature, all men are born free." Nevertheless, Jefferson lost the case, and the man remained a slave.

Jefferson was a member of the House of Burgesses when the new crisis with Britain hit the colonies. Earlier, he had listened at the door of the Virginia capitol's chamber to Patrick Henry denounce the Stamp Act, but now he was inside the chamber as a delegate. Under pressure from the colonial boycott of British goods, Britain had repealed the Stamp Act in 1766. However, now the British were imposing new taxes on glass, lead, tea, and paper. They were also cracking down harder on those colonists who avoided paying their taxes or who traded illegally. Once more, angry colonists boycotted British goods.

The protests were especially strong in the Boston area, so the British sent two army regiments there to keep order. Jefferson had not been in the Assembly long when he got to join his fellow legislators in voting their support for the Massachusetts colony. When the new governor found out about the vote, he had the doors of the Assembly locked to show his disapproval. The legislators, Thomas Jefferson among them, moved down the street to the Raleigh Tavern and held their meetings there. Once more they voted to boycott British goods to protest the new taxes. And once more the protest of Virginia and other colonies worked. The British government gave in and repealed all the 1767 taxes, except the one on tea. Peace returned to the colonies, at least for the time being.

Jefferson thought about his own future and began to

make preparations for the day when he would have his own family. Even though he had spent years in the colony's capital of Williamsburg, he decided he wanted to live on the land he had grown up on and not in some town or city. In accordance with his father's will, he had chosen for himself an elevated piece of family property across the river from Shadwell. He named it Monticello (Italian for "little mountain") and decided it was where he was going to settle down. He leveled the top of the hill and sank a deep well. Although he didn't yet know whom he was going to live with there, he began to design and build the house that would be his home for the rest of his life.

When Jefferson was twenty-seven, he met and fell in love with Martha Wayles Skelton, a young widow who lived in Charles City County near Williamsburg. She had a son by her first husband, who had died suddenly after only twenty-two months of marriage. The love of music she and Jefferson shared was one of the things that drew them together. She played the harpsichord and sang too. A story goes that when Jefferson was courting Martha at her home, two other young men arrived to pay their respects. But when they heard the two of them singing together so happily, they went away knowing they had no chance.

The wedding took place in Martha's home on New Year's Day, 1772, and two weeks later the couple set off for their new home. It was a hundred miles to Monticello, and

Monticello,
Jefferson's home

the last part of their journey was on horseback through a heavy snowstorm. But they finally arrived at Monticello and began their marriage and life together. Despite much hardship and tragedy—the death of Martha's little son and three of their own six children, and Martha's own illnesses—these ten years were generally happy ones for Jefferson.

REVOLUTIONARY
POLITICS

—4—

For the first two years of his marriage, Jefferson was busy with family matters, his law practice, and the building of Monticello. He continued his work on the main house, and around it he added a garden, orchard, and deer park. He and Martha had two daughters: the first they named Martha and the second Jane Randolph, after Jefferson's mother, who lived across the river at Shadwell.

When Martha's father died eighteen months after she married Jefferson, she inherited 135 slaves and 11,000 acres of land. Added to the 50 slaves and the more than 5,000 acres Jefferson already owned, he had to spend more of his time managing this new property, and so had less time to practice law. Anyway, travel over back roads was difficult and time-consuming and too many of his clients were not paying their fees. When revolutionary ferment virtually closed the courts in Virginia, he gladly gave up law for politics.

Jefferson's choice of reading materials at this time shows that his mind was very much on the problems the colonies were having with Britain. He ordered books from England in large quantities. He devoured the writings of John Locke on government and philosophy, and he read the works of Newton, Bacon, and other thinkers. He read all he could about the revolts and revolutions of history to find out what caused them.

In 1773, a dramatic new crisis between Britain and her American colonies erupted over tea. The British government decided to let the East India Company dump its surplus tea on the American market. Because the company was allowed to sell its tea tax-free to American storekeepers, the British thought they were doing the colonists a favor. But they were wrong. American tea merchants resented the competition from the cheaper tea and the favoritism shown the East India Company. Also, to exempt them from the tea tax only reminded Americans that the tea tax still applied to them.

When the tea arrived in American ports, the colonists refused to unload it. In Boston the fiery rebel Sam Adams took the protest one step further. On the night of December 16, he and his friends dressed up like Indians and boarded one of the ships. Then, as a crowd watched and cheered, they lifted the chests of tea and dumped them overboard.

News of this "Boston Tea Party" spread rapidly through the colonies. In London an angry British government moved

Martha Jefferson

The "Boston Tea Party"

quickly to punish Boston. They closed down the port until all the tea was paid for, and they refused to let the Massachusetts legislature meet. They also sent over a general with his troops to govern the colony. These "intolerable acts," as the colonists called them, fired up the colonists and did more than anything else to unite American feelings against Britain.

In Virginia the governor dissolved the House of Burgesses and tried to prevent a new one from meeting. The Virginia colonists decided to hold a convention of their own. Albemarle County reelected Jefferson to serve as a delegate, but he fell ill on the way and had to turn back. He did manage to have the resolutions he worked on at Monticello sent on to the convention, where they were later published. Without his knowledge, Jefferson's words were printed in Williamsburg as "A Summary View of the Rights of British America." Although it was only twenty-three pages long, his summary expressed brilliantly the complaints of the American colonists against the British Parliament and king. Virginia lawmakers were so impressed that when they chose their delegation to the First Continental Congress in Philadelphia, which included such better-known Virginians as George Washington and Patrick Henry, they made Jefferson a deputy delegate.

Then, when one of the Virginia delegates returned, Jefferson, at thirty-two, got his chance to join the congress of colonial leaders that John Adams called "a collection of the greatest men on this continent." Jefferson already knew Washington and Henry from Virginia, but in Philadelphia he got to meet for the first time other colonial leaders such as Sam and John Adams of Massachusetts and Benjamin Franklin of Philadelphia.

Although there were only six weeks left in the session when he got there, Jefferson was put on several committees, where he quickly impressed his older colleagues. Once again, he hardly ever spoke up in public debate, but he was tireless in his committee work. John Adams made special note in his diary of the young man who "has learned French, Italian, Spanish, and wants to learn German." Later he wrote that Jefferson brought to the Congress a "reputation for literature, science, and a happy talent of composition . . . he was so prompt, frank, explicit, and decisive upon committees and in conversation that he soon seized upon my heart." That was the beginning of a friendship between the two men that was to last a lifetime. (More than fifty years later, they died on exactly the same day.)

Jefferson worried a great deal about his family when he was away from them. Back home at Monticello during his first break from Congress, he experienced the death of his younger daughter, Jane Randolph, who was only one and a half. He also learned how deeply the conflict with Britain was dividing his mother's side of the family. One of his cousins, Peyton Randolph, whom Jefferson admired greatly, was a revolutionary leader in Virginia and in Congress, but another cousin, John Randolph, who was the attorney general of Virginia, was so pro-British that he sold his land and property and moved to England, although he could not get his son to join him.

Jefferson attended the fall session of the Congress, but when he was home again he met with yet another tragedy. On the last day of March, 1776, his mother suffered a stroke and died. He was supposed to return to Philadelphia, but his mother's death affected him so deeply that he became ill and for weeks suffered a series of severe migraine headaches. After he finished mourning his mother's death and recovered his health, he returned to Philadelphia for what turned out to be one of the most productive periods in his life.

THE DECLARATION
OF INDEPENDENCE AND
A NEW GOVERNMENT
FOR VIRGINIA

5

By the spring of 1776, the Revolutionary War was under way and there seemed to be no turning back. Congress selected George Washington to lead the American forces, and by March he had been able to force the British to leave Boston.

In May and June, Jefferson was back with Congress in Philadelphia, but he wondered if he was in the right place. In Williamsburg the Virginia legislators were meeting in convention to create a new government. They had already instructed Jefferson and the rest of the Virginia delegation in Congress to propose that Congress declare the colonies free and independent. Now in anticipation of self-government, the Virginia legislators in Williamsburg were hard at work creating a new constitution. Jefferson saw this work as the really important task and regretted that he could not be back in Virginia sharing in it.

However, while he was in Philadelphia he drafted a state constitution that he sent to the Virginia convention by way of his friend and former law teacher, George Wythe. Unfortunately, it did not arrive in time. Another version was adopted, but parts of Jefferson's were added as amendments. Also, the list of charges against King George III that Jefferson had carefully prepared was used as the new constitution's preamble.

Many Americans still favored making peace with Britain, and Congress even sent the king an "Olive Branch Petition" that assured him of their loyalty and promised to restore good relations if his unjust laws were repealed. Others favored immediate separation. Congress decided to postpone a final decision until the beginning of July, but, for the meantime, it selected a committee to prepare for the possibility of separation.

On June 11 Congress elected five of its members and charged them with the most momentous assignment ever given in the history of America: the drafting of a formal declaration of independence from Great Britain. Jefferson won the most votes, even more than John Adams and Benjamin Franklin. By now the drafting skills of the young Virginian were well known and widely appreciated. Jefferson thought Adams should be the one to do the actual writing, but Adams declined, telling Jefferson that he would do a much better job.

In seventeen days—from June 11 to June 28, when the committee reported to Congress—Jefferson composed the Declaration of Independence that today is famous around the world. Although Adams and Franklin made suggestions, this extraordinary declaration of human freedom was Jefferson's own work.

He did not consult a book or pamphlet when writing it. His only direct borrowing was from his own list of charges against the king that he sent to the Virginia convention. Everything else came straight from his mind and heart. The origins of his thinking went back to his reading about politics and government that he had begun at the College of William and Mary. The philosophy of John Locke had been especially important. Locke believed that people had natural rights that no government should ever try to deny. Even kings needed the "consent" of their subjects.

In the Declaration of Independence Jefferson wrote:

We hold these Truths to be self-evident, that all Men are created equal, that they are endowed by their Creator with certain unalienable Rights, that among these are Life, Liberty, and the Pursuit of Happiness—That to secure these Rights, Governments are instituted among Men, deriving their just Powers from the Consent of the Governed. . . .

This was a revolutionary idea—that governments were meant to serve people, not the other way around. Jefferson went on to say that if any government tried to take away or abuse these natural rights of its citizens, that government

Benjamin Franklin, Thomas Jefferson, Samuel Adams, and others drafting the Declaration of Independence

IN CONGRESS, JULY 4, 1776.

The unanimous Declaration of the thirteen united States of America.

When in the Course of human events, it becomes necessary for one people to dissolve the political bands which have connected them with another, and to assume among the powers of the earth, the separate and equal station to which the Laws of Nature and of Nature's God entitle them, a decent respect to the opinions of mankind requires that they should declare the causes which impel them to the separation.

We hold these truths to be self-evident, that all men are created equal, that they are endowed by their Creator with certain unalienable Rights, that among these are Life, Liberty and the pursuit of Happiness.—That to secure these rights, Governments are instituted among Men, deriving their just powers from the consent of the governed,—That whenever any Form of Government becomes destructive of these ends, it is the Right of the People to alter or to abolish it, and to institute new Government, laying its foundation on such principles and organizing its powers in such form, as to them shall seem most likely to effect their Safety and Happiness. Prudence, indeed, will dictate that Governments long established should not be changed for light and transient causes; and accordingly all experience hath shewn, that mankind are more disposed to suffer, while evils are sufferable, than to right themselves by abolishing the forms to which they are accustomed. But when a long train of abuses and usurpations, pursuing invariably the same Object evinces a design to reduce them under absolute Despotism, it is their right, it is their duty, to throw off such Government, and to provide new Guards for their future security.—Such has been the patient sufferance of these Colonies; and such is now the necessity which constrains them to alter their former Systems of Government. The history of the present King of Great Britain is a history of repeated injuries and usurpations, all having in direct object the establishment of an absolute Tyranny over these States. To prove this, let Facts be submitted to a candid world.

He has refused his Assent to Laws, the most wholesome and necessary for the public good.

He has forbidden his Governors to pass Laws of immediate and pressing importance, unless suspended in their operation till his Assent should be obtained; and when so suspended, he has utterly neglected to attend to them.

He has refused to pass other Laws for the accommodation of large districts of people, unless those people would relinquish the right of Representation in the Legislature, a right inestimable to them and formidable to tyrants only.

He has called together legislative bodies at places unusual, uncomfortable, and distant from the depository of their public Records, for the sole purpose of fatiguing them into compliance with his measures.

He has dissolved Representative Houses repeatedly, for opposing with manly firmness his invasions on the rights of the people.

He has refused for a long time, after such dissolutions, to cause others to be elected; whereby the Legislative powers, incapable of Annihilation, have returned to the People at large for their exercise; the State remaining in the mean time exposed to all the dangers of invasion from without, and convulsions within.

He has endeavoured to prevent the population of these States; for that purpose obstructing the Laws for Naturalization of Foreigners; refusing to pass others to encourage their migrations hither, and raising the conditions of new Appropriations of Lands.

He has obstructed the Administration of Justice, by refusing his Assent to Laws for establishing Judiciary powers.

He has made Judges dependent on his Will alone, for the tenure of their offices, and the amount and payment of their salaries.

He has erected a multitude of New Offices, and sent hither swarms of Officers to harass our people, and eat out their substance.

He has kept among us, in times of peace, Standing Armies without the Consent of our legislatures.

He has affected to render the Military independent of and superior to the Civil power.

He has combined with others to subject us to a jurisdiction foreign to our constitution, and unacknowledged by our laws; giving his Assent to their Acts of pretended Legislation:

For Quartering large bodies of armed troops among us:

For protecting them, by a mock Trial, from punishment for any Murders which they should commit on the Inhabitants of these States:

For cutting off our Trade with all parts of the world:

For imposing Taxes on us without our Consent:

For depriving us in many cases, of the benefits of Trial by Jury:

For transporting us beyond Seas to be tried for pretended offences:

For abolishing the free System of English Laws in a neighbouring Province, establishing therein an Arbitrary government, and enlarging its Boundaries so as to render it at once an example and fit instrument for introducing the same absolute rule into these Colonies:

For taking away our Charters, abolishing our most valuable Laws, and altering fundamentally the Forms of our Governments:

For suspending our own Legislatures, and declaring themselves invested with power to legislate for us in all cases whatsoever.

He has abdicated Government here, by declaring us out of his Protection and waging War against us.

He has plundered our seas, ravaged our Coasts, burnt our towns, and destroyed the lives of our people.

He is at this time transporting large Armies of foreign Mercenaries to compleat the works of death, desolation and tyranny, already begun with circumstances of Cruelty & perfidy scarcely paralleled in the most barbarous ages, and totally unworthy the Head of a civilized nation.

He has constrained our fellow Citizens taken Captive on the high Seas to bear Arms against their Country, to become the executioners of their friends and Brethren, or to fall themselves by their Hands.

He has excited domestic insurrections amongst us, and has endeavoured to bring on the inhabitants of our frontiers, the merciless Indian Savages, whose known rule of warfare, is an undistinguished destruction of all ages, sexes and conditions.

In every stage of these Oppressions We have Petitioned for Redress in the most humble terms: Our repeated Petitions have been answered only by repeated injury. A Prince whose character is thus marked by every act which may define a Tyrant, is unfit to be the ruler of a free people.

Nor have We been wanting in attentions to our British brethren. We have warned them from time to time of attempts by their legislature to extend an unwarrantable jurisdiction over us. We have reminded them of the circumstances of our emigration and settlement here. We have appealed to their native justice and magnanimity, and we have conjured them by the ties of our common kindred to disavow these usurpations, which, would inevitably interrupt our connections and correspondence. They too have been deaf to the voice of justice and of consanguinity. We must, therefore, acquiesce in the necessity, which denounces our Separation, and hold them, as we hold the rest of mankind, Enemies in War, in Peace Friends.

We, therefore, the Representatives of the united States of America, in General Congress, Assembled, appealing to the Supreme Judge of the world for the rectitude of our intentions, do, in the Name, and by Authority of the good People of these Colonies, solemnly publish and declare, That these United Colonies are, and of Right ought to be Free and Independent States; that they are Absolved from all Allegiance to the British Crown, and that all political connection between them and the State of Great Britain, is and ought to be totally dissolved; and that as Free and Independent States, they have full Power to levy War, conclude Peace, contract Alliances, establish Commerce, and to do all other Acts and Things which Independent States may of right do.—And for the support of this Declaration, with a firm reliance on the protection of divine Providence, we mutually pledge to each other our Lives, our Fortunes and our sacred Honor.

John Hancock

Button Gwinnett
Lyman Hall
Geo Walton

Wm Hooper
Joseph Hewes,
John Penn

Edward Rutledge.

Thos Heyward Junr.
Thomas Lynch Junr.
Arthur Middleton

Samuel Chase
Wm Paca
Thos Stone
Charles Carroll of Carrollton

George Wythe
Richard Henry Lee
Th Jefferson
Benj Harrison
Thos Nelson jr.
Francis Lightfoot Lee
Carter Braxton

Robt Morris
Benjamin Rush
Benj. Franklin
John Morton
Geo Clymer
Jas. Smith
Geo. Taylor
James Wilson
Geo. Ross
Caesar Rodney
Geo Read
Tho M:Kean

Wm Floyd
Phil. Livingston
Frans. Lewis
Lewis Morris
Richd. Stockton
Jno Witherspoon
Fras. Hopkinson
John Hart
Abra Clark

Josiah Bartlett
Wm Whipple
Saml Adams
John Adams
Robt Treat Paine
Elbridge Gerry
Step. Hopkins
William Ellery
Roger Sherman
Sam'el Huntington
Wm Williams
Oliver Wolcott
Matthew Thornton

must be changed or abolished. In a world in which kings ruled by divine right, this was a radical point of view.

Using the catalog of complaints he sent to Virginia, Jefferson listed in detail the charges against the king, describing the many ways he had abused American liberties. The document concluded with a ringing revolutionary declaration of freedom:

> We, therefore, the Representatives of the UNITED STATES OF AMERICA . . . do, in the Name, and by Authority of the good People of these Colonies, solemnly Publish and Declare, That these United Colonies are, and of Right ought to be, FREE AND INDEPENDENT STATES; that they are absolved from all Allegiance to the British Crown, and that all political Connection between them and the State of Great-Britain, is and ought to be totally dissolved. . . .

When, after heated debate, Congress voted the adoption of this document and signed it on July 4 (thereafter celebrated as the nation's "birthday"), the break with Britain was complete. Even though the war to establish that freedom had only begun, this act of Congress created "the United States of America."

Nevertheless, that summer Jefferson's heart was still in Virginia. Not only was he concerned that his influence on

The signed Declaration
of Independence

the making of the new state government was weakened by his not being back at the convention, but he was also very worried about Martha. She was pregnant again, and, because of her problems with childbearing, he wanted to be at her side when she gave birth. He asked to be relieved of his duties, but his replacement was slow in coming. He finally was able to leave Philadelphia on September 3, but that was too late. Before he could reach her, Martha, who was staying at her sister's house in Virginia, suffered a miscarriage.

For the next three years (1776–1779), Jefferson remained in Virginia working to make his new state more democratic. As a member of the state's House of Delegates, he drafted many new laws. He also headed the committee chosen to revise completely the colonial law code. Happily, he could do much of this work at home in Monticello, where he could be near his ailing wife. By the time he finished his work in 1779, he had created a new body of laws that was the basis of a sweeping and radical transformation of the nature of society. These laws touched every possible subject, from the most local matter to the larger issues of citizenship, crime, slavery, religion, and education. Jefferson, in his own words, "laid the axe to the root of pseudo-aristocracy" and described his four major bills as "a system by which every fibre would be eradicated of ancient or future aristocracy and a foundation laid for a government truly republican."

Many of the laws Jefferson proposed were not passed while he was still in the legislature. Instead, they were enacted later with the help of friends such as James Madison, who believed in his ideas. Some of his most advanced ideas, like his bill to emancipate the slaves, were never adopted.

One of Jefferson's proudest accomplishments was the law he drafted for religious freedom. He had always regarded religion as a strictly private matter, and maintained that every person should be free to believe whatever he wanted to. Jefferson was tolerant of all religions and thought it was not the business of government to favor one over the other. He wrote: "But it does me no injury for my neighbor to say that there are twenty gods, or no god. It neither picks my pocket nor breaks my leg."

His bill called for the separation of church and state, and later it became a model for the rest of the nation. In colonial Virginia there wasn't religious freedom because there was an established church—the Church of England. This meant that the church received special privileges and that everyone had to pay taxes to support it, even people who belonged to other churches or practiced other religions. People who did not belong to the established church could not hold public office.

Jefferson's fight for religious freedom was deeply rooted in his passionate conviction that the human mind must be free and that truth must not be coerced. Thoughts and beliefs should not be under the jurisdiction of government. Truth should stand on its own, and, if it is allowed to do so, it will win out in the end. This was stated in his bill:

> . . . that Almighty God hath created the mind free; that all attempts to influence it by temporal punishments or burdens, or by civil incapacitations, tend only to beget habits of hypocrisy and mean-

ness . . . and, finally, that truth is great and will prevail if left to herself; that she is the proper and sufficient antagonist to error, and has nothing to fear from the conflict, unless by human interposition disarmed of her natural weapons, free argument and debate; errors ceasing to be dangerous when it is permitted freely to contradict them.

Of all of his battles in the House of Delegates, this one against the power of the established church and its clergy was Jefferson's toughest. He considered his bill for religious freedom one of the greatest achievements of his life. He was so proud of it he requested it be mentioned on his tombstone.

THE WAR YEARS

—6—

To Jefferson and the people of Virginia, the fighting in the north seemed distant. After the American victory over the British at Saratoga in 1777 and the French entry into the war on the American side, Jefferson was sure that the war was going well and would be over soon. His first contact with the enemy was civil, even friendly. Four thousand British and Hessian (German) troops captured at Saratoga were marched nearly 700 miles (1,130 km) south to Albemarle County for safekeeping. Jefferson made friends with them, especially the German officers. He discussed philosophy with one of them and played a violin duet with another. When the authorities allowed the wife of the highest ranking Hessian officer and his three daughters to join him, Jefferson had them all over to dinner at Monticello.

However, Jefferson soon got a truer picture of war when the British shifted their military effort to the South. The Virginia legislature elected Jefferson war governor in

June, 1779. That meant that suddenly he was in charge of defending an area larger than Great Britain that had a long coastline and many rivers where the British could attack. With the threat of a British invasion by sea, the state government had been moved up the James River from Williamsburg to a more central location, at Richmond, but this wasn't far enough. Benedict Arnold, an American general who went over to the British side, advanced up the James River with a huge invasion force, while General Cornwallis led his troops against Richmond from the south. Jefferson moved the government from Richmond to Charlottesville, but the British kept coming. With the state government in flight, the British swarmed the countryside. They destroyed one of Jefferson's farms and briefly occupied Monticello.

This was a terrible time for Jefferson. He was war governor during the two years when the British invaded, and his term ended just at the time their invasion was most successful. Moreover, Martha had lost two of her last three children, and she barely recovered from her last birth. And if his flight from the British just as his term as war governor expired wasn't humiliating enough, he was thrown off his horse and laid up for six weeks.

Jefferson's "retirement" could not have come at a worse time. The British were still overrunning the state, and the surrender of Cornwallis at Yorktown that ended the war was still months away. Although he later admitted that he had been "unprepared by [my] line of life and education for the command of armies," he had made the best of an impossible situation in which he had to perform his job with a never-ending shortage of money, troops, weapons, and supplies. Still, he was hurt when the legislature voted to investigate his conduct as governor during the crisis. In

The capitol of Virginia at Richmond

Richmond Jefferson spent two weeks explaining the difficulties Virginia faced and the actions he took to ease them. His reputation was restored, but later his enemies tried to use his war record against him.

After his two years as governor, Jefferson wrote what was later to be published as a book. A French diplomat, who was seeking information about the different states that made up the United States, sent Jefferson a set of twenty-one questions. Jefferson's detailed answers grew into essays which in turn grew into chapters of a lengthy work. He arranged to have the manuscript delivered to the Frenchman in the spring of 1782.

Jefferson did not write his work with the intention of having it published, but later, when he was in France, it was published as *Notes on the State of Virginia*. Nobody knew Virginia better than Jefferson did; he had lived there all his life and his father had surveyed much of it. His work gives a complete description of the geography, commerce, agriculture, and natural and social history of Virginia, whose territory at the time extended far out into the west. In one part of the book, Jefferson provides detailed information about American animals and proves they were not smaller versions of European ones, as some Old World scholars claimed. Today Jefferson's book is regarded as an American classic. One scholar has called it "one of America's first permanent literary and intellectual landmarks . . . probably the most important scientific and political book written by an American before 1785."

Jefferson resigned his seat in the Virginia legislature after it cleared his name and gave him a vote of thanks for his "ability, rectitude and integrity." He also declined to serve in the Continental Congress. He was too worried about his family to venture too far from home. Not only was Martha pregnant again, but, after the death of his good friend Dabney Carr, he took his sister Martha and her six children into his own family. When his wife gave birth to a baby girl, whom they named Lucy Elizabeth after the little girl they lost the year before, Jefferson had nine children to provide for.

Martha was only thirty-three, but she was not able to recover her health after her latest childbirth. She never left her bed, clinging to life for several months, while Jefferson, his sister, and his sister-in-law took turns nursing her. Then, as Jefferson recorded in his account book for September 6, 1782: "My dear wife died this day at 11:45 A.M."

Jefferson was devastated. He retreated to his room and didn't come out for three weeks. His daughter Martha was his only companion. Then, when he did leave his room, he would take long rides on his horse through the woods. Only six weeks after his wife's death did he emerge from what he later described as a "stupor of mind" that had left him "dead to the world."

There was a story passed down by his slaves that while his wife was on her deathbed, Jefferson promised her he would never marry again. We can't be certain if this story is true. What we do know is that Jefferson, who was thirty-nine, never did remarry, even though he lived for more than forty more years.

When he was elected to the new Congress, he agreed to serve. Although unhappy and not in the best health himself, he plunged into his congressional work and accomplished a great deal. In six months he drafted thirty-one important papers. He devised the plan that provided self-government for the western territories and established the procedure for them to become states. He also reformed the country's coinage by establishing a decimal system based on the dollar. Nonetheless, he was restless. He found Congress to be bogged down with petty squabbling. Therefore, when he was asked to go to Paris to help Benjamin Franklin and John Adams make treaties with the nations of Europe, he accepted gladly.

FRANCE

-7-

Paris, the glittering capital of France, was very different from the worlds of Monticello and Williamsburg. Paris was the intellectual center of the world, and eventually Jefferson would become part of its vibrant life. But it would take him many months to emerge from its lonely fringes.

When Jefferson went to Paris, he took along a twenty-five-year-old Virginian named William Short to be his private secretary, and his daughter Martha, whom he thought old enough to benefit from a French education. He left his two youngest daughters, Polly and little Lucy, with their aunt in Virginia. After he set up his household, he put Martha in a Catholic convent school that had an excellent reputation among diplomats.

Benjamin Franklin was already famous in Europe, and the French adored him. Adams and Jefferson met regularly at his house to plan how to win respect for the United States in the eyes of France and the other European nations.

These meetings reunited the three men who had been most responsible for the Declaration of Independence, but this time their job was to earn recognition and commercial rights for the young republic.

Jefferson became a frequent visitor to the house of John and Abigail Adams and their children. Also, the French nobleman Lafayette, who had done so much to help the American Revolution, and his wife did much to help Jefferson feel at home in Paris. But even the efforts of his friends and the sights and sounds of the city could not lift him out of the gloom that settled in after he lost his wife. Then came the shattering news from home: little Lucy had died of whooping cough. Jefferson remained in poor health and depressed spirits during his first winter in Paris.

However, the longer he stayed in Paris, the better he liked it. By spring, he was writing his friends, Madison and Monroe, to visit him in the summer. He began shipping books by the dozen to Madison, who was to play such an important role in the creation of the American Constitution. Madison devoured everything Jefferson sent him. In return, Madison sent Jefferson long letters informing him about political developments in the United States. The best news of all came in late 1786, when Madison wrote that the Virginia legislature had finally passed, without changing it substantially, Jefferson's bill for religious freedom.

Jefferson's stay in France provided the richest years of his life. He was already highly civilized and wise about the ways of the world before he set out for Paris, but his understanding of people and ideas matured in Europe. He listened attentively to political leaders, writers, and intellectuals of all points of view. He spent hours wandering among secondhand bookstalls along the Seine River to buy and read treasured volumes of classical and Renaissance literature. He met the leaders of French society and became a favorite in the most intellectual and influential salons of Paris.

In 1785, after Franklin departed for home and Adams became America's first ambassador to England, Congress made Jefferson the American ambassador to the French court. This meant that he represented the United States at Versailles, the vast royal estate with its huge palace and great fountains, gardens, and parks. Just to appear before the king and his court, Jefferson had to spend hours having his hair dressed. However, he never had any illusions about what he could accomplish there; he reported sadly that at the French court, the American ambassador was "among the lowest of the diplomatic tribe."

Jefferson's one diplomatic trip to England ended in failure. When Adams presented him at court, King George III received the two Americans ungraciously in front of the entire diplomatic corps. The king may have been trying to let the author of the Declaration of Independence know what he thought of him, but Jefferson felt that the insult was not so much directed against him personally as against the young American republic. Jefferson never did like the English, and this incident only confirmed to him what he felt was England's continued hostility to its former colony.

In Paris Jefferson worked tirelessly to win respect for America and to secure better trading rights with European nations. As a generous host, he made many French friends for himself and for his country, and he also served as a host for Americans who visited Paris.

Jefferson's longest trip outside Paris was the four-month journey he made by himself through southern

France and northern Italy. Always the curious observer, he took in all he could and made extensive notes about farming, bridges, boats, canal locks, wines, and many other special features of the countryside. For example, after spending a whole day in an Italian dairy, he made detailed notes about the making of Parmesan cheese. He was always thinking about ways to improve life back home. He sent olive trees and a promising strain of rice to South Carolina because he was sure that state had the right climate for them.

Along the way he talked to as many of the common people as he could; he knocked on the doors of peasants and talked with them for hours about how they lived and what they thought. Walking along a road once, he struck up a conversation with a poor ragged woman who made only eight sous (about eight cents) a day as a laborer and had two children to feed. Sometimes, when there was no work, they had to go hungry. Jefferson later wrote that he walked with her for almost a mile (1.6 km). "I gave her on parting twenty-four sous. She burst into tears of gratitude, which I could perceive was unfeigned because she was unable to utter a word." By the time he got back to Paris, he knew more about the people of France than any other foreign ambassador and most of the officials of the French court as well.

Jefferson decided he wanted his six-year-old daughter, Polly, with him in Paris too, but getting her there turned out to be quite a job. Every time he wrote to try to persuade her to come, she wrote back telling him she was quite happy with her aunt and uncle and cousins in Virginia. She said she had no desire to cross the ocean and suggested that if he and Martha wanted to see her, they should come to Virginia. Finally, at Jefferson's urging, she had to be brought to the ship and tricked into staying on it while it left. She was delivered to Abigail Adams in England and grew so attached to her that she didn't want to leave her either. The servant Jefferson sent to fetch her there had to carry her off bodily. When she arrived in Paris, she barely recognized her father, and she didn't know her fifteen-year-old sister at all. But before long, she felt at home with them. Jefferson put her into the convent school with Martha, where she became an immediate favorite.

As the American ambassador, Jefferson was in a unique position to witness the beginnings of the French Revolution and the events that led up to it. He was optimistic that France could proceed peacefully "step by step to a new constitution." He attended the opening of the Estates-General that the king was forced to summon in May, 1789, but he was skeptical that such a large body—1,200 nobles, clergy, and commoners—could accomplish much. His French friends tried to get him to help devise a constitution, but he knew that his place as a foreign diplomat was to remain in the background. As crisis followed crisis and the Paris mobs took charge of the streets, Jefferson grew more and more concerned. Nonetheless, despite the problems, by the time he left Paris in October, 1789, Jefferson was still optimistic about France's future.

SECRETARY
OF STATE

—8—

When Jefferson set sail for America, he didn't think he was leaving France permanently. His plan was to return home for several months to settle his daughters back in Virginia and to take care of his farms and debts. Then he was going to return to Paris, where he was sure he could cement good relations between the United States and the emerging revolutionary government of France.

When he arrived in the port of Norfolk, he was surprised to read in the newspaper that President George Washington was going to appoint him secretary of state in the new government. On his way back to Monticello, a formal letter from Washington caught up with him. Jefferson's first reaction was negative, but Washington kept after him. Jefferson's friend James Madison convinced him that the new government and the country needed him. Therefore, he accepted, and he never returned to Paris.

After several months of putting his affairs at home in order, he settled Polly once more with her beloved aunt. (Martha married a young, handsome Virginian by the name of Thomas Mann Randolph.) Then he headed north to New York, stopping off on the way in Philadelphia to visit the ailing Benjamin Franklin for what proved to be his last meeting with the great man.

In New York City, Jefferson rented a small house on Maiden Lane and went to work immediately with a staff of two chief clerks, two assistant clerks, and a translator. The secretary of state was not only responsible for the foreign affairs of the young nation, but he was also in charge of Indian affairs, weights and measures, patents, lighthouses, and many other things. Jefferson's first big job was a complete report on weights and measures that would have put the United States on the metric system at the beginning of its history had Congress had the foresight to accept it.

The longer Jefferson was in New York, the more shocked he became by the talk he heard at the dinners of the leaders of New York society. In contrast to the views of the French revolutionary patriots that he favored, Jefferson found that these wealthy Americans had little faith in democracy or in "the people." They admired the very system of aristocratic privilege whose corruption and decline he had witnessed in Europe. New York City had remained in British hands throughout the war, so there was still a good deal of pro-British sentiment. For these antidemocrats, the British form of government was the one they admired most.

The hero of these wealthy bankers and merchants was the young, cocky Secretary of the Treasury, Alexander

Hamilton. He had outlined a bold, ambitious plan to repay the federal debt, which was hurting American credit all over the world. Although Jefferson agreed something needed to be done, he worried that with Hamilton's help this new aristocracy of wealth and privilege might dominate the new government.

Part of Hamilton's plan to set the finances of the country in order was to have the federal government absorb all the war debts of the states. Madison was the leader of the opposition to this idea in Congress, so Jefferson brought Hamilton and Madison together for dinner at his house, and an agreement was worked out. In exchange for Madison's help in passing his bill, Hamilton agreed to lend his support to the idea of a "federal city" on the banks of the Potomac. To get the bill through Congress, the help of the Pennsylvania delegation was needed, so the final compromise allowed the nation's capital to be in Philadelphia for the ten years it would take to clear the land for and build the yet-to-be-named Washington, D.C.

Washington had always dreamed of having the national capital on the Potomac, not far from where he lived. He made Jefferson, whose architectural interest and skill were well known, his unofficial assistant for planning and constructing the new capital. Jefferson had the new city laid out in the classical style that he most loved, a style that emphasized the space, order, and dignity that visitors to Washington, D.C., find today.

The more Jefferson got to know Hamilton, the more troubled he was by the man's aristocratic tendencies and his open admiration of the British and their form of government. Hamilton did not think the mass of people should rule themselves; rather they should be ruled over by the

Washington, D.C., as it looked during Jefferson's time. The President's House—later to be known as the White House—is slightly to the left of center.

rich and wellborn. One evening at dinner, Jefferson was shocked when Hamilton announced that the man he admired most in history was the Roman general and dictator Julius Caesar.

The two men divided over the issue of Hamilton's Bank of the United States. Hamilton's plan was to stabilize the currency by creating a national bank modeled on the Bank of England, but Jefferson and Madison thought it was unconstitutional and would benefit mainly the wealthy northerners who surrounded Hamilton. Jefferson argued that such a bank was not provided for explicitly in the Constitution. However, Congress did pass the bank bill, and, over Jefferson's objections, Washington signed it into law. Hamilton was now convinced that Jefferson was his archenemy.

When the government moved to Philadelphia, Jefferson found high society there as extravagant, and sentiment in favor of Hamilton and the British as strong, as it had been in New York. While Jefferson attended the dinners of the fashionable upper class as part of his duty as an important government official, he much preferred the company of scientists and thinkers such as David Rittenhouse, president of the American Philosophical Society.

The political controversy began to heat up in the newspapers. Philip Freneau, who agreed with the republican principles of Jefferson and Madison, began publishing the *National Gazette* in Philadelphia, in whose columns he at-

Alexander Hamilton.
He and Jefferson differed
on many issues.

tacked Hamilton and accused him of wanting to turn the United States into a monarchy. Hamilton defended himself by going on the offense. Using the columns of a New York newspaper that favored his policies and those of his followers (already beginning to be called Federalists), he assailed Freneau and the man he saw behind it all—Thomas Jefferson. This newspaper war raged back and forth until Jefferson had been called just about everything, including "the most intriguing man in the United States" and "a revolutionary who hid behind the garb of a modest, retiring philosopher."

Jefferson told President Washington that he wanted to resign at the end of Washington's first term, which was only six months away. He told the president that the prospect of this kind of mudslinging was the reason he had hesitated about accepting the post in Washington's government in the first place. However, Washington convinced him that it was important to him personally and to the country for Jefferson to stay on the job. Jefferson stayed on.

RETREAT
AND RETURN

—9—

Americans followed the news from France closely. From the beginning they had been sympathetic to the revolution that seemed so much like their own—a struggle of the people against the tyranny of the king. They rejoiced when the king was overthrown and a republic established. And when the armies of the kings of Austria and Prussia attacked France to put down the revolution and restore the king to his throne, they applauded the news of the early French victories. However, when the French put their king on trial for treason and then cut off his head, many Americans thought that was going too far. But when America's old enemy England joined the other kings against France, most Americans rallied once more to the side of the French.

With France and England now at war, the United States had to decide what to do, and as usual Jefferson and Hamilton were on different sides of the issue. In the meetings in the president's office, Hamilton was pro-British, while Jefferson argued that America should not abandon its closest ally, France, which had done so much to help it win its own revolution. Washington decided on a policy of neutrality. In public Jefferson defended that policy, but in private he remained a staunch defender of the French and their revolution.

Jefferson's job of defending the French was made harder by people such as the new French ambassador, Edmond Genêt. At first Jefferson thought he was charming and reasonable, but he soon discovered Genêt was really demanding and arrogant. Genêt insisted that the United States should repay immediately all the money it had borrowed from France during the American Revolution. He also set out to make illegal purchases of American ships for the French war effort. He even insulted President Washington by threatening to go over his head to the American people to get him to change his policy.

Once more Jefferson and Hamilton clashed over what to do about this troublesome Frenchman. Jefferson convinced the president that the best course was not to condemn him in public and offend France, but rather to write to the French government explaining the problem and requesting that he be recalled. The writing of this letter turned out to be Jefferson's last act as secretary of state. He was determined to return to Virginia, and this time Washington couldn't talk him out of it. On the last day of 1793, Jefferson submitted his formal resignation, and a few days later set off for home.

For the next three years Jefferson happily lived the life of the gentleman farmer. Surrounded by his two daughters, his first two grandchildren, his books, and a steady stream of visiting relatives and friends, he supervised the cultivation of his fields and rebuilt Monticello to three times its original size. He moved his library, which he called "the best in America," from the second to the first floor and replaced the roof of the mansion with a dome. He also improved the surrounding landscape by expanding his vineyard and adding weeping willows, fig trees, and strawberry beds.

Yet at no time during this period was the world of politics very far from his mind. Madison wrote to him as often as three times a week from Philadelphia, and Monroe and other Republicans corresponded with him regularly. With the approach of the presidential election of 1796, they were convinced that Jefferson was the only one who had a chance to lead the Republicans to victory. Washington announced that under no circumstances would he run for a third term. When it looked as if the Federalists were going to put forward Vice President John Adams as their candidate, the Republicans turned to the retired scholar-recluse of Monticello to be their candidate.

During the campaign, both Jefferson and Adams remained above the battle. Neither outlined his policies nor said anything negative about the other. But in speeches and newspapers across the land, their followers more than made up for their civility with scathing attacks and slander. Jefferson was accused of everything from atheism to cowardice. When the French ambassador said France might have to declare war on the United States if Jefferson wasn't elected, many Americans resented his interference.

On the Federalist side, Alexander Hamilton was trying to manipulate the outcome of the election behind the scenes. Since he didn't like Adams, he tried to throw the election to the Federalist vice presidential candidate from South Carolina. In those days each state elector got two votes, so by conniving with the Federalist electors in South

Carolina not to vote for Adams, the vice presidential candidate would end up with more votes and become president. Hamilton's scheme might have worked had it not been exposed by Aaron Burr, Jefferson's vice presidential candidate from New York.

The race was very close: Adams carried the North, Jefferson the South, and they divided the states in between. But Adams won 71 electoral votes to Jefferson's 68. Jefferson had already made up his mind that, in the event of a tie, he planned to step aside for his old friend. In fact, when the final vote was in, he seemed relieved. He wrote to a friend, "I have not ambition to govern men." Nonetheless, by coming in second he had been elected vice president.

Jefferson hesitated about making the long trip to Philadelphia for his inauguration, hoping that there might be some way for him to take the oath of office at Monticello. However, he finally decided to brave the mud and ice, partly because the vice presidency of the country was not the only office he was going to accept in Philadelphia. The president of the American Philosophical Society, David Rittenhouse, had died, and this elite group of the nation's most accomplished philosophers and scientists decided that only Thomas Jefferson would be a worthy successor.

After he was sworn in to both offices, Jefferson presented to the society a scientific paper on an ancient giant sloth recently discovered in a Virginia cave. Jefferson brought the bones with him to Philadelphia and used their enormous size to once more challenge the argument of a famous French scientist of his day who claimed that the animals of Europe were larger than those of America. Without knowing it, Jefferson was helping found the science of paleontology.

VICE PRESIDENT
AND PARTY LEADER

— 10 —

In Philadelphia in his capacity as vice president, Jefferson emerged as leader of the Republican opposition. Madison had played that role for years, but he was now in temporary retirement in Virginia. Soon the Republicans were put in an uncomfortable position by the new French government. It decided to stop all ships, American ones included, that might be carrying British goods. When President Adams sent a strong denunciation of France to Congress, the Republicans accused the Federalists of trying to provoke a war with France and demanded to see the correspondence with the French government.

Adams gladly made the letters public. When the newspapers printed them, the country was shocked by the picture of French arrogance. Because he had been offended that American policy now seemed to be favoring the British, the French foreign minister, Talleyrand, had demanded from the United States a huge loan—and a $250,000 bribe as well! Although the American ambassador had refused to give in to the demands of Talleyrand's agents (designated X, Y, and Z), the revelation of these XYZ papers whipped the country up into an anti-French frenzy. Jefferson and the Republicans were denounced in the press and even in the streets. Jefferson could only stand by helplessly as he watched Congress scrap its treaty of friendship with France and raise an army and navy in preparation for war.

In this atmosphere of hysteria, the Federalists moved to silence their critics. They pushed through Congress the Naturalization Act and the Alien and Sedition Acts, designed to curb dissent. Since they didn't like the way new immigrants rushed to join the Republicans, the Federalists passed the Naturalization Act, which increased the years required to become a citizen from five to fourteen. The Alien Act gave the president the authority to expel any alien he judged "dangerous to the peace and safety of the United States." French and Irish refugees who had fled from their own troubled countries now had a much harder time becoming American citizens, and, if they were too critical of the government, they could be sent back.

The Sedition Act made it a crime for anyone to make a "false, scandalous, and malicious" statement or publish anything "against the government of the United States." This law meant that the Federalists could muzzle the Republican press. Twenty-five people were arrested under the act, including four Republican editors and members of Congress.

Although Jefferson remained calm and urged his followers to do the same, he knew that the Federalists were watching him closely, and that any provocative statement or action on his part could get him arrested. He and Madison met secretly in Virginia and devised a plan for states in which Republicans were strong to protest these hateful acts. They each agreed to write a set of resolutions to be submitted to the legislature of a state. However, Jefferson's role in this plan had to be kept secret because, as the nation's vice president, he could be accused of treason if his participation were discovered. A friend of Jefferson's was to deliver his resolutions to the North Carolina legislature, but when he read how strong and explosive they were, he decided that he could entrust them only to his brother in the Kentucky legislature.

The passing of both sets of resolutions in Kentucky and Virginia had an immediate impact. They signaled the Federalists and the nation as a whole that there was a limit to the power of the Federalists and that plenty of people disapproved of their acts. These resolutions marked the turning of the tide, as it soon became evident in the election of 1800.

This time Jefferson was willing and ready for the battle ahead. Convinced that nothing less than the future of freedom in America was at stake, he prepared for what he believed was to be the most important battle of his life. Night after night he met with his followers and Republican leaders around the country to plan strategy and create the first political party in American history. With painstaking care he organized the Republicans state by state, with designated leaders organizing each state's political groupings all the way down to the neighborhood level. Then, with the campaign organized and the Republicans ready to carry the fight to every farm and hamlet, Jefferson returned to Monticello for what turned out to be the nation's dirtiest campaign so far.

The attacks against Jefferson became so vicious that Adams defended him, much to the consternation of the Federalists. Adams said Jefferson was "the man in the United States fittest to be President." Hamilton was so fed up with Adams by now that he wrote a scathing letter against Adams's "disgusting egotism" that was made public. This attack by the leader of the Federalists against his own candidate sank whatever chances President Adams had for reelection.

In the election of 1800, Jefferson and his Republican running mate, Aaron Burr, ended up with the same number of votes. In the case of a tie, the decision had to be made by the House of Representatives. The House had just moved with the rest of the Federal government to the new capital of Washington, which at the time was little more than a clump of buildings set in the wilderness. For the next week, Washington became the scene of high political drama, as the Federalists tried to block Jefferson's election by making Burr president instead.

While the House remained deadlocked ballot after ballot, day after day, the country waited anxiously. Restless crowds roamed the streets and rumors of civil war filled the air. Finally, one week later, a key Delaware delegate switched his vote, and several other Federalists followed. Thomas Jefferson was elected president of the United States. The infant republic had made it safely through its worst crisis, but the country Jefferson inherited was badly divided.

PRESIDENT
(FIRST TERM)

-11-

On the morning Jefferson was to be inaugurated, he entered the dining room of Conrad's boardinghouse and sat down for breakfast at the end of the table. When the wife of a senator from Kentucky offered him her seat at the head of the table, he declined politely, saying he preferred his usual place. This incident shows that from the beginning Jefferson was determined to do away with the pomp and ceremony that had become a part of the Federal government under Washington and Adams.

At noon, dressed "like a plain citizen without any distinctive badge of office," Jefferson walked to the Capitol and delivered to Congress and a packed gallery of spectators his inaugural address. In a speech that he regarded as his most important statement since the Declaration of Independence, he appealed to the divided nation for reconciliation and reason. He reminded the country of the great principles it stood for—justice, peace, free elections, majority rule, minority rights, payment of debts, civilian control of the military, and freedom of religion, press, assembly, and speech. What united them was much stronger than what divided them, he said. "We are all Republicans—we are all Federalists."

However, the atmosphere of party politics and personal attack continued, and the campaign of slander against Jefferson that had begun earlier seemed to get even worse. Much of it came from one man—a troubled Virginia journalist, James Callender, whom Jefferson had once tried to help financially. However, when Jefferson did not submit to Callender's demand for a postmastership, Callender turned on him and attacked him viciously. He traveled throughout Virginia to pick up every piece of gossip that had ever been whispered about Jefferson and then printed it in his newspaper. His juiciest charge was that Jefferson had a secret slave mistress with whom he had fathered several children. The Federalists gladly circulated the story and went so far as to claim that this young, pretty slave was "the queen of Monticello." Jefferson refused to be drawn into the bitter controversy, but he didn't try to censor the press either, the way the Federalists had done. Jefferson believed that eventually truth would win out: "I laid it down as a law to myself, to take no notice of the thousand calumnies issued against me, but to trust my character to my own conduct, and the good sense and candor of my fellow citizens." Callender continued his bitter attacks until he finally drank himself to death.

Under Jefferson, the White House was much more open to the public than before. He stopped the twice-a-week formal receptions Washington and Adams used to hold for foreign dignitaries and government officials; instead, he opened the White House every morning to any citizen who wanted to visit. Jefferson dressed as simply as he lived. Much to the displeasure of the pompous British ambassador, Jefferson refused to dress up for important people any more than he would for the average citizen. One amazed Federalist returned from his first White House visit and recorded in his diary: "A tall, high-boned man came into the room; he was drest, or rather undrest, with an old brown coat, red waistcoat, old corduroy small clothes, much soiled—woolen hose—slippers without heels. I thought this man was a servant . . . It was the President."

The one day Jefferson did make a special fuss about was the Fourth of July. Once, when a group of citizens came to the White House to find out when his birthday was so they could celebrate it, he told them the only birthday he ever celebrated was the country's. Every year on the Fourth he organized a parade on the White House lawn and then invited everyone in afterward for cakes, wine, punch, and lemonade. With the marine band playing in the hall, Jefferson stood at the door of the White House and shook the hand of every visitor who entered.

At first, Jefferson found life in the White House lonely, despite the dinners and receptions. Except for his private secretary, Meriwether Lewis, he was the only one who lived there. He was always trying to get his daughters and grandchildren to visit him. He felt better when his two sons-in-law were elected to Congress in 1802 and agreed to live with him in the White House.

On the political front, he was able to undo much of the Federalists' work. He repealed the Judiciary Act, which had allowed President Adams to appoint many new Federalist judges just before he left office. He let the hated Alien and Sedition Acts expire, and he gradually repealed the whiskey tax and other taxes the Federalists had enacted. Also, with the help of his secretary of the treasury, he began reducing the national debt by three million dollars a year.

Even while Jefferson reduced the size of the armed forces, which the Federalists had built up for a war that never happened, he did put the navy and marines to good use against the Barbary pirates. For years, the pirates, controlled by the ruler of Tripoli, had been harassing American ships and extorting money from the United States government. So Jefferson sent the U.S. Navy to the Mediterranean. When American ships blockaded Tripoli from the sea, the ruler gave in and agreed to negotiate a peace treaty.

Jefferson's greatest foreign policy success was the Louisiana Purchase. That vast territory comprised a million square miles that stretched from New Orleans north to the Canadian border and included the heartland of the continent between the Mississippi River and the Rocky Mountains. France had ceded it to Spain in 1763, but now that Napoleon controlled Spain, it was rumored that the enormous expanse of land had been ceded back to France.

Jefferson, who saw the importance of the Mississippi valley to the future of American commerce and expansion, was determined to keep France from controlling the great Mississippi River. Through diplomatic channels he urged France to cede New Orleans at the mouth of the Mississippi to the United States and threatened to make an alliance with the British if it didn't. He sent James Monroe to Paris to assist the American ambassador with the negotiations. Much to the Americans' surprise, the French wanted to discuss the sale of the entire Louisiana territory, not just New Orleans. When the bargaining was over, the greatest real estate deal in American history had been concluded: for $12,000,000 (about 2¢ an acre), the United States was suddenly twice as big.

Jefferson and the rest of the nation were jubilant. When he informed Congress that no new taxes would be needed to pay the bill for the purchase because of savings the government had made, Jefferson's popularity soared. In the election of 1804, he carried every state except Connecticut and Delaware. Even Massachusetts, the home of John Adams and long a bastion of Federalism, voted for Jefferson. His decisive victory—162 to 14 in the electoral college—pleased him greatly.

PRESIDENT
(SECOND TERM)

-12-

Jefferson began his second term with peace at home and abroad, but before long he had to deal with the problem of Aaron Burr. When the Republicans nominated Jefferson for a second term, they dumped Burr. During his vice presidency, he had flirted with the Federalists after nearly beating Jefferson out for the presidency with their support. The Republicans chose another candidate for vice president and didn't give Burr a single vote.

To regain political power in his home state of New York, Burr ran for governor. When he tried to gain Federalist support, Hamilton denounced him as "a dangerous man." After Burr lost, he charged Hamilton with "base slanders" and challenged him. Hamilton accepted, thus setting the stage for the famous duel that took place in Weehawken, New Jersey, just across the Hudson River from New York. On that fateful morning of July 11, 1804, Burr's shot struck Hamilton down, and he died the next afternoon. Under indictment for the shooting in New York and New Jersey, Burr fled south. For Jefferson, his troubles with his former vice president were just beginning.

Burr traveled through the South and West to raise a secret army to fight the Spanish. He even got General Wilkinson, the commander in chief of the army that Jefferson sent to occupy New Orleans, interested in his plan. Burr told people his goal was to liberate Florida and Mexico from Spanish rule, but his real dream was evidently to establish an empire in the West with New Orleans as the capital and himself as ruler.

When Jefferson received reports about Burr from the West, he ordered gunboats to New Orleans and instructed western officials to watch Burr closely. When General Wilkinson developed cold feet about Burr's scheme, he wrote to Jefferson about his "deep, dark, wicked and widespread conspiracy." Jefferson immediately issued a proclamation condemning Burr and called on all governors of the western states and territories to keep Burr's army from assembling. Overnight Burr's troops dispersed, and he and his lieutenants were arrested.

Burr was brought to trial for treason, but Jefferson's Federalist opponents, including Chief Justice John Marshall, rallied to his defense. Burr was acquitted, but Jefferson had the satisfaction of seeing that the trial transcripts—deeply incriminating to Burr—were published by Congress. To escape the bad publicity and his mounting debts, Burr was forced to flee to Europe.

Much better news from the West arrived when it was reported to Jefferson that Lewis and Clark had returned from their expedition across the continent. It was really Jefferson's expedition: he had planned and organized it and had gotten Congress to finance it. Also, he had chosen its leader—his private secretary, Meriwether Lewis, who in turn chose the experienced frontier soldier, William Clark. Jefferson arranged to have Lewis coached in astronomy, botany, mineralogy, cartography, zoology, and Indian history.

In the spring of 1804, the two young Virginians set off up the Missouri River with about forty soldiers, two interpreters, and a black servant. Later, they were joined by an Indian squaw named Sacajawea. Two and a half years later they returned to St. Louis after having crossed the continent and reached the Pacific Ocean. When Jefferson heard the news, he was delirious with joy. Several weeks later he addressed Congress about the great accomplishments of the expedition and what it meant for the future of the country.

Jefferson's own interest in scientific learning remained as strong as ever. As president of the American Philosophical Society, he was in touch with scientists in the United States and Europe. In the White House East Room he displayed various inventions and relics. He invented many gadgets for use around the White House, too, such as a rotating clothes rack and circular shelves.

Jefferson was very attached to his grandchildren. He did not think they visited him enough, and when they did, he played with them endlessly. When they were back home in Virginia, he wrote each one of them regularly. After the death of his beloved daughter, Polly, he seemed to cling all the more to Martha and his grandchildren.

Toward the end of his second term, Jefferson was forced to issue an embargo that prohibited American ships from entering foreign ports. The policy was directed against

*Jefferson sent the explorers Lewis and Clark
on an expedition across the continent.*

the British and the French, who were interfering with American ships, but the embargo ended up hurting Americans as well. That gave the Federalists a new excuse to attack Jefferson, but even the Republicans and Jefferson himself were not completely satisfied with the effects of the embargo.

In 1808 Jefferson declined to run for a third term, but he made no secret of his choice for a successor—his long-time friend and political ally, his secretary of state, James Madison. When Madison and the Republicans scored an overwhelming victory in the election, Jefferson felt pleased that he was leaving the government in good hands. After attending Madison's inauguration, he packed his belongings and wrote to a friend, "Never did a prisoner released from his chains feel such relief." Then, on March 11, 1809, happy to be returning home at last, Thomas Jefferson rode out of Washington, never to return.

James Madison was a close friend and political ally of Jefferson's.

THE FINAL YEARS

—13—

At home, surrounded by his many grandchildren, Jefferson settled happily into his new life. He attended to his debts and his farms, he continued to improve Monticello, and he received the steady stream of relatives, friends, and curious strangers who came to visit. Most of the visitors Jefferson enjoyed, but the rest he just didn't have the heart to turn away. Since hospitality was a way of life in Virginia, and there was no inn nearby, visitors, even strangers, were put up at Monticello, by then a thirty-five room mansion. Later, Martha remembered that they sometimes had fifty guests at a time.

When he needed to, Jefferson could get away. At Monticello he often retreated to his private quarters off the entrance hall. There in his study, library, and bedroom, he had complete privacy. No one could enter without an invitation, not even Martha or the grandchildren. In the summer he used to escape the crowds by going off with his youngest granddaughters to the small house he built on his Bedford County property ninety miles away.

Jefferson loved his library and read by candlelight every night. "I cannot live without books," he often said. Even so, after the British burned the small congressional library when they raided Washington, D.C., during the War of 1812, Jefferson offered his own extensive library as a replacement. Congress agreed to buy his library, and Jefferson's books became the new foundation for what is today the Library of Congress.

Although his interest in political affairs continued and many asked him for advice, Jefferson was careful not to interfere in the administrations of his two friends who followed him in the presidency—James Madison and James Monroe. When a rift developed between the two men in the election of 1808, Jefferson healed the split. As a result, Madison appointed Monroe his secretary of state, thus making him the Republican heir apparent to the presidency.

Jefferson carried on an enormous correspondence. In 1820 alone he received 1,267 letters. He answered almost all the mail he received and kept copies of all his letters. At the time of his death he had left in his files about 38,000 letters—both those he had received and copies of those he had sent. Historians were always writing to him to clear up questions about the people and the events of the Revolutionary era, and he answered their questions as honestly as he could. In the interests of history he even wrote his autobiography up to the French Revolution, but that's as far as he got. "I am tired of talking about myself," he said.

Jefferson was not one to hold grudges, and many of

The Library is divided into 44 chapters, the system of classification was originally prepared by president Jefferson, but has been modified since. It is based upon lord Bacon's division of knowledge, the subject classed according to the faculties of the mind employed on them.

the letters he wrote were meant to heal old political wounds. One of his greatest satisfactions was the resumption of the friendship with John Adams that politics had injured. After exchanging cautious greetings through a mutual friend, the two old political warriors took up their pens and began what became a great correspondence in American history. For fourteen years until the end of their lives, they wrote each other about everything from politics to philosophy, religion, history, and the mysterious ways of nations and peoples. Jefferson and Adams discovered that their political views were closer than they had thought, and they ended up holding each other in the highest esteem and affection.

At the age of seventy-four, Jefferson began the great project of his final years—the founding of the University of Virginia. He had been concerned with education and educational philosophy all his life, but no more so than during these last years. Jefferson considered knowledge not only a means to an end, but an end in itself, to be enjoyed for its own sake. Not only was education the key to virtue and happiness, it was the basic necessity for self-government. Freedom could neither flourish nor survive without educated citizens, he believed.

All his life Jefferson had worked to safeguard people's liberties. Only when people were free from religious dictation, political tyranny, and personal persecution could their

*The library classification system
prepared by Jefferson*

minds be free to pursue knowledge and cultivate learning. Fear and prejudice were the enemies of democracy, so that educational facilities open to all were crucial for an effective and well-organized society. Thus, in his retirement, Jefferson reopened his campaign for general education in Virginia, the cornerstone of which was to be a state university. This university, he believed, could be the greatest achievement in his lifetime, dedicated to the belief that truth makes people free.

The University of Virginia, which was the first great university of the South and the first American university to be free of an official church connection, was his daily concern. But to become reality his idea had to go through several stages. After he got a small academy in Charlottesville upgraded to a college, Jefferson persuaded the Virginia legislature to make the college into the new state university. Using Madison, now retired after his two terms as president, as his righthand man, Jefferson pressured the legislature to come up with the necessary money year after year. He personally surveyed the grounds, designed the buildings, and even supervised the construction of the first buildings. Despite a small budget, he hired an excellent faculty, mostly from Europe.

When the university finally opened in March, 1825, Jefferson was naturally its first rector. Soon after the new students arrived, Jefferson had them all to dinner at Monticello and continued that practice two or three times a week. The students loved to hear his stories about the great events of the Revolutionary period a half a century earlier, and Jefferson made no secret of his love for these conversations with the students. A friend of his once said that the

The creation of the University of Virginia was the most significant example of Jefferson's total commitment to education.

two things Jefferson loved most were "old books and young minds."

By riding his horse for an hour or two every day, Jefferson retained his amazing vigor. Nonetheless, his last years were difficult ones. After he fell ill in the fall of 1818, he was never again free of pain. Because of declining farm income and increasing debts, he also had to worry about losing Monticello. He sold property and took out bank loans, but each year the situation got worse. Finally, his grandson had to organize a lottery in the north to save Monticello from the auction block.

Jefferson continued to receive visitors, including Lafayette, who returned to a hero's welcome in the United States. But the terrible strain of his financial crisis took its physical toll. When, in March, 1826, a urinary disease began draining his strength, Jefferson drew his final will, which provided for the freedom of five of his ablest and most faithful slaves. By June he was too weak to get out of bed. On July 2, knowing that the end was near, he called his family to his bedside and told them he wanted them to live true and honest lives.

Jefferson died at Monticello on July 4—the fiftieth anniversary of the Declaration of Independence and the same day John Adams died in Massachusetts. The next day Jefferson was buried under the great oak tree on Monticello's hillside next to his wife and daughter.

Jefferson's sketch and instructions for his tombstone

could the dead feel any interest in Mon
-ments or other remembrances of them, when, a
Anacreon says: Ολιγη δε κεισομεσθα
Κονις, οσεων λυθεντων
the following would be to my Manes the mos
gratifying.
On the grave
a plain die or cube of 3.f without an
mouldings, surmounted by an Obelisk
of 6.f. height, each of a single stone:
on the faces of the Obelisk the following
inscription, & not a word more
"Here was buried
Thomas Jefferson
Author of the Declaration of American Independan
of the Statute of Virginia for religious freedo
& Father of the University of Virginia"

because by these, as testimonials that I have lived, I wish most to
be remembered. ~~to be~~ to be of the coarse stone of which
my columns are made, that no one might be tempted
hereafter to destroy it for the value of the materials.
my bust by Ciracchi, with the pedestal and truncated
column on which it stands, might be given to the University
if they would place it in the Dome room of the Rotunda.
on the Die of the Obelisk might be engraved

On his gravestone the family chiseled the epitaph he had requested:

HERE WAS BURIED THOMAS JEFFERSON

AUTHOR OF THE
DECLARATION
OF
AMERICAN INDEPENDENCE

OF THE
STATUTE OF VIRGINIA
FOR
RELIGIOUS FREEDOM

AND FATHER OF THE
UNIVERSITY OF VIRGINIA

*A fitting tribute to one
of the most exceptional
founders of our country—
the Jefferson Memorial
in Washington, D.C.*

FOR
FURTHER READING

Brodie, Fawn. *Thomas Jefferson; An Intimate History*. New York: Norton, 1974.

Fleming, Thomas. *The Man from Monticello; An Intimate Life of Thomas Jefferson*. New York: William Morrow, 1969.

Koch, Adrienne, and William Peden, eds. *The Life and Selected Writings of Thomas Jefferson*. New York: Random House, 1944.

Malone, Dumas. *Jefferson and His Time*, 6 vols. Boston: Little Brown, 1948–1981.
    Jefferson the Virginian (I)
    Jefferson and the Rights of Man (II)
    Jefferson and the Ordeal of Liberty (III)
    Jefferson the President: First Term, 1801–1805 (IV)
    Jefferson the President: Second Term, 1805–1809 (V)
    The Sage of Monticello (VI)

Peterson, Merrill D. *Thomas Jefferson and the New Nation*. New York: Oxford University Press, 1970.

INDEX

ABOUT
THE AUTHOR

Charles Patterson grew up in New Britain, Connecticut. A graduate of Amherst College and Columbia University (Ph.D.), he has taught history and literature in junior high and high school, as well as in college and adult education programs. Now an editor and writer in New York City, he is a member of The Authors Guild. His first book, *Anti-Semitism: The Road to the Holocaust and Beyond* (Walker, 1982), was for young adult readers.